GRAPHIC HISTORY

THE Pilgrims AND THE First Thanksgiving

by Mary Englar
illustrated by Peter McDonnell

Consultant:

Melodie Andrews, PhD
Associate Professor of Early American History
Minnesota State University, Mankato

Capstone
press

Mankato, Minnesota

Graphic Library is published by Capstone Press,
1710 Roe Crest Drive, North Mankato, Minnesota 56003.
www.capstonepub.com

Library of Congress Cataloging-in-Publication Data
Englar, Mary.
    The Pilgrims and the first Thanksgiving / by Mary Englar; illustrated by Peter McDonnell
    p. cm.—(Graphic library. Graphic history)
    Includes bibliographical references and index.
    ISBN-13: 978-0-7368-5492-4 (hardcover)
    ISBN-10: 0-7368-5492-4 (hardcover)
    ISBN-13: 978-0-7368-9656-6 (softcover pbk.)
    ISBN-10: 0-7368-9656-2 (softcover pbk.)
    1. Pilgrims (New Plymouth Colony)—Juvenile literature. 2. Massachusetts—History—New
Plymouth, 1620-1691—Juvenile literature. 3. Thanksgiving Day—Juvenile literature. I. Title. II.
Series.
F68.E55 2007
974.4'02—dc22   2006014724

Summary: In graphic novel format, tells the devastating story of the Pilgrims' first year in
America up until their Harvest Festival.

Designer
Jason Knudson

Editor
Mandy Robbins

Editor's note: Direct quotations from primary sources are indicated by a yellow background.

Direct quotations appear on the following pages:
Pages 7, 11, 20, from *Of Plymouth Plantation: 1620–1647* by William Bradford (New York:
Random House, 1981).

Printed in the United States of America in Stevens Point, Wisconsin.
082012   006879R

Table of Contents

7

Shortly after signing the peace treaty, Governor Carver became ill and died. William Bradford became the new governor.

We must carry on Governor Carver's dream of a colony in the New World.

The *Mayflower* crew left for England on April 5, 1621. Not a single one of the Pilgrims went back to England.

Squanto stayed with the Pilgrims for many months. He taught them how to survive in the new world.

This stream is full of herring.

CHAPTER 4

The Harvest Feast

The young colony grew stronger. By autumn, the settlers had a bountiful corn crop.

Never have I seen such a good crop.

Squanto, you are a special gift from God sent to help us.

My people celebrate to thank the Creator for such harvests.

Governor, do you think we might have a Harvest Feast?

It is an English tradition, after all.

Yes. I think Governor Carver would have enjoyed a Harvest Feast.

23

The celebration included more than eating. The Pilgrims and the Wampanoag showed their skills with weapons and played competitive games.

THWACK!

THUNKK!

They are very accurate!

When the feast was over, the Wampanoag returned to their village. The Pilgrims began preparing for their second winter.

Mother, it's getting cold. Will we be hungry again this winter?

No, dear. This winter we will have food and warm houses. The coming year will be much better than the last.

Plymouth Colony grew to 2,000 people by 1640. In 1691, Plymouth joined the Massachusetts Bay Colony.

MORE ABOUT THE

Pilgrims
AND THE
First Thanksgiving

 The people we know as Pilgrims had separated from the Church of England. They were called Separatists. Being a Separatist was against the law in England.

 The Separatists of Plymouth called themselves "Saints." When William Bradford wrote a book about the colony years later, he called them Pilgrims because they traveled a long way for religious freedom.

Giving thanks was a central part of life for American Indians. They had held thanksgiving feasts for hundreds of years before the Pilgrims arrived.

 The Pilgrims called their first autumn festival the Harvest Feast. To them, a day of thanksgiving meant a day of prayer, with no eating at all.

 Squanto stayed with the Pilgrims until he died of an illness in 1622.

 The peace treaty between Governor Carver and Chief Massasoit lasted for more than 50 years.

Soon after the Pilgrims came to Massachusetts, people called Puritans moved there from England. Their religious beliefs were similar to the Pilgrims' beliefs. But the Puritans stole the Indians' land and tried to force their way of life on them. In 1675, Massasoit's son, Philip, went to war against all the white settlers. In 1676, the white settlers defeated the local Indians and took their land.

 In 1863, President Abraham Lincoln declared the last Thursday in November as Thanksgiving Day. In 1941, President Franklin D. Roosevelt changed the date to the fourth Thursday in November.

 The food enjoyed at the Pilgrims' Harvest Feast was not what most Americans eat when celebrating Thanksgiving. The Pilgrims' meal included deer, fish, and other seafood. If they had turkey at all, it was wild turkey. Potatoes, cranberry sauce, and pumpkin pie were not served at all.

Glossary

Pilgrim (PIL-gruhm)—one of the English Separatists or other colonists who settled in North America in 1620

Separatist (SEP-uh-rah-tist)—one of a group of British people who wanted to practice religion separately from the Church of England

translate (TRANS-late)—to change one language into a different one; Squanto could speak both English and Wampanoag, so he translated for the Pilgrims.

treaty (TREE-tee)—an agreement between two groups of people to be peaceful

FactHound offers a safe, fun way to find Internet sites related to this book. All of the sites on FactHound have been researched by our staff.

Here's how:
1. Visit *www.facthound.com*
2. Choose your grade level.
3. Type in this book ID **0736854924** for age-appropriate sites. You may also browse subjects by clicking on letters, or by clicking on pictures and words.
4. Click on the **Fetch It** button.

FactHound will fetch the best sites for you!

Read More

Davis, Kenneth C. *Don't Know Much About the Pilgrims.* New York: HarperCollins, 2002.

Grace, Catherine O'Neill, and Margaret M. Bruchac with Plimoth Plantation. *1621: A New Look at Thanksgiving.* Washington, D.C.: National Geographic Society, 2001.

Plimoth Plantation. *Mayflower 1620: A New Look at a Pilgrim Voyage.* Washington, D.C.: National Geographic Society, 2003.

Santella, Andrew. *The Plymouth Colony.* We the People. Minneapolis: Compass Point Books, 2001.

Bibliography

Bradford, William. *Of Plymouth Plantation: 1620–1647.* New York: Modern Library, 1981.

Bradford, William, and Edward Winslow. *Mourt's Relation or Journal of the Plantation at Plymouth.* New York: Garrett Press, 1969.

Deetz, James, and Patricia Scott Deetz. *The Times of Their Lives: Life, Love, and Death in Plymouth Colony.* New York: W.H. Freeman, 2000.

Winslow, Edward. *Good Newes from New England.* Bedford, Mass.: Applewood Books, 1996.

Index